Original title:
A Chronicle of Womanhood

Author: Luise Luik
Editor: Jessica Elisabeth Luik
ISBN 978-9916-39-241-6

A Chronicle of Womanhood

Luise Luik

Iron wrapped in Ivory

Iron clad, courage never frail,
Embedded in Ivory's enchanting veil.
Two forces intertwined, ever so grand,
Unseen by those who fail to understand.

In each strife, they speak to the night,
While casting spells under the moonlight.
Resilience and grace, an arcane amity,
In a world that favors brute audacity.

Forge and feather, together they write,
A tale of valor, burning bright.
For Iron wrapped in Ivory tells the tale,
Of a courage that never, ever fails.

Sisters of the Solstice

Sisters of the Solstice, bathed in golden light,
Their voices harmonizing with the silent night.
Their shadows danced and pranced upon the gleaming snow,
As Church Bells echoed mirth, a Yule's festivity to show.

Through hushed whispers and silent prayers,
The sisters conjured up celestial layers.
Their magic strung across the wintry sky,
As stardust fell softly, a cosmic lullaby.

They wove dreams with threads of the milky way,
In rhythm with the Earth's harmonic sway.
Sisters of the Solstice, bearers of the light,
Guiding lost souls through the Winter's night.

Pearls from the Past

Pearls of the past, rich with wisdom's glow,
Each a treasured keepsake, reflecting time's flow.
Ancestral voices whispering tales old yet gold,
A narrative bound by time, waiting to be told.

Through fleeting moments and centuries' sigh,
The pearls of wisdom never lie.
They speak of battles fought and won,
Of kinship formed under the setting sun.

Their tranquil glow warms the silent abyss,
In their reflection, a timeless bliss.
Pearls from the past, their luster won't ever die,
Keeping alive our roots, under the cosmic sky.

Woman's Woven Walkways

Through unmarked paths and hidden gateways,
Are the tales of woman's woven walkways.
Each thread intricately spun in the loom of time,
A testament of struggle, yet a sublime chime.

Her journey mapped in fabrics fine,
Each stitch a symbol, each fold a line.
Telling tales of grace, and silent might,
Journeys undertook with radiant light.

Through realms unseen and lands untold,
The woman journeys, fierce and bold.
Her woven walkway, a work of art,
An emblem etched deep in the heart.

Lantern Lit Legacy

Underneath the moon's mystic glow,
In the heart's uncharted meadow,
Illuminated by lantern's light, dancing slow,
Are the stories tossed in the shadows.

Lantern burning through the untold night,
Guiding footsteps, a knight's bright legacy,
Through woods darkened, love's sacred fight,
In every echo, words of prophecy.

In the lantern's flickering flame so bold,
A thousand tales quietly unfold,
Stories of valour, new and old,
Legacy etched in heart, never to be sold.

In the silent whispers of twilight's end,
A lantern lit legacy, our divine friend,
Guiding our path as we ascend
Tales of love to time we lend.

The Sapphire Skyline

Above the smoke, rise buildings tall as lore,
Set against the sapphire skyline, forever more,
Washed with twilight hues and lost stars once bore,
A canvas painted in dreams, from cosmic store.

In the beautiful ascent of the moon,
In the sapphire skyline, we find our tune,
Bathed in the silver light of a celestial boon,
Each spangled night and radiant noon.

We dance on precipices, under the sapphire sky,
Each heart a soaring comet, passers-by,
Inking lines of poems that fly,
In the constellation of us, hung high.

Scenes set in dreams, the undying kind,
In sapphire skyline, what stories you'll find,
Each whispering wind, each love unrefined,
In the sapphire poetry, woven in mind.

The Buds of Becoming

Tiny buds of hope, tightly packed,
In the heart's fertile soil, delicately tracked,
Bursting forth in spring's sweet act,
In the story of becoming, beautifully exact.

Unfurling petals of promised potential,
In the garden of life, remarkably essential,
Fragrance of dreams, ever sequential,
The buds of becoming, exceedingly influential.

Tiny buds, kissed by the sun's earnest ray,
Emerging bravely in the existential ballet,
The symphony of life, in splendid display,
Buds of becoming in the heart's bouquet.

Unseen forces guide their graceful unfurling,
In whispers of wind, love's message hurling,
The seeds of tomorrow in today's swirling,
The buds of becoming, constantly twirling.

The Feminine Flame

In realm of shadows, a flame abides,
A feminine essence, that in every heart resides,
Burning fiercely, undying tides,
An eternal beacon that ever guides.

Birthed from stars, in cosmos spun,
The feminine flame, equal to none,
A melodic shriek that has been sung,
Since the aged moon, around us, begun.

A tender strength, from sacred core,
The feminine flame, an opened door,
Burning brighter, forever more,
In every heart, a lustrous lore.

In weave of universe, a tapestry,
The feminine flame, wild and free,
In whispers of wind, call of sea,
The echo of us, the echo of she.

Portrait of Pearlescent Passion

In moonlit dreams and silent screams,
A passion-driven vessel teems.
Under stars that e'er sparkle bright,
Shines a pearl, with internal light.

A flood of passion stirs the sea,
Lost in an endless, moonlit spree.
In the sea's dance, beneath the mien,
A ripple of pearlescent sheen.

An echo softly, roaring high,
Shattered whispers across the sky.
Imbuing heartbeats in the deep,
In pearls, secrets they quietly keep.

Upon the brooks, a tale is spun,
Of a passion burning brighter than sun.
Cast in a matchless, brilliant light,
The portrait of pearlescent might.

Ballad of Unbound Beauty

In bows of the sunrise, the song of creation,
Resides a melody, of unbound elation.
A ballad it weaves, through the wind's soft sigh,
Sings the feeling of beauty, under the sky.

The beauty uncaged, in its rightful decree,
Mirrors the free spirit, dancing with glee.
Humbled by nature, yet proudly stands tall,
A beauty untethered, answers its call.

In the rustle of leaves, on the sigh of a breeze,
The ballad of beauty, plays with ease.
In the heart of the wild, sings in tranquility,
A tune of love, and boundless felicity.

Beneath the moon's glow or sun's golden veil,
The beauty of life, tells a wondrous tale.
The ballad lives on, in whispers and roars,
A testament to beauty, that ever soars.

Wine-stained Wisdom

In vino veritas, truth in deepest crimson hue,
In drops of wisdom, grace washed anew.
Unveiled are secrets, under the spreading vine,
Beneath its tendrils, truth and falsehood intertwine.

In every drop, poignant tales behold,
Lost echoes of histories, untold.
From rim to heart, a truth does reside,
In the macroscope within the wine-stained tide.

Every sip a sentence, every gulp an age,
Wine-stained histories on memory's page.
In every note, in every taste, wisdom's footprints traced,
Glossed in truth, in deep wine encased.

In the cacophony of life, amongst the prattle and din,
The wisdom bestowed by wine-stains within,
Though noble hearts may err and roam,
In the wine-stained wisdom, they find their way home.

Canvas of Courage

Upon the canvas, brushed and untamed,
Where fear is named, and courage claimed.
Through layers of trials, in battles well fought,
The paintbrush shapes, tales courage has wrought.

In fiery hues of might and red,
The canvas breathes, stories left unsaid.
Etched in bold strokes and somber signs,
The embodiment of courage, in every line.

A symphony of fearless acts, reveals,
In the silence of the canvas, courage appeals.
An undaunted image, in every hue,
A testament to bravery, resolute and true.

Transcending boundaries, crossing the ridge,
The canvas of courage, paints the bridge.
A striking portrait of bravery's stand,
In the strokes of courage, we understand.

Echoes of Emerald

In the caverns of memory, silent and old,
Lit by the emeralds' ever enchanting hold,
Residing in shadows, tales yet untold,
Echoes of emerald, brave and bold.

Their voice, soft whispers in the hush of gold,
The moonlight waxes, nocturnal and cold,
Serenading lost stories of the marauder's mould,
In the echoes of emerald, secrets unfold.

Through the hallways of heart, the echoes resound,
In the eyes of a stag, solaces are found,
In mother's love, life is intricately wound,
Echoes of emerald, in love, they're crowned.

And in the quietest chambers of the night's hold,
Whispers of Potter stories never grow old,
In their courage, we forever them enfold,
Echoes of emerald, forever bold.

In Ink and Ivory

Of words crafted in ink and ivory so pure,
Spelt tales of enchantment, enduring allure,
In the realm of dreams, where truths endure,
Ink painted stories, magic the cure.

Ballads of bravery, in knight's grandeur,
Fairy tales spun, in quaint lanquetry's lure,
Caught in ink and ivory, memories assured,
Silent whispers of fiction, humanity's cure.

Inscribed in parchment, heart's disclosure,
Printed pages echoing unspoken composure,
In the arsenal of wit lies the wizard's power,
In ink and ivory, let the imagination tower.

In the dance of quill on the page so fine,
In tales enchanting, as old as time,
We resonate with tales, in every line,
In ink and ivory, our dreams intertwine.

Unfolding the Umbrella of Utopia

In shades of dreams yet unspoken,
Unfolds the umbrella of Utopia, token,
Beneath its shade, hearts unbroken,
Where hope blooms, words golden.

Beneath the canvas painted fair,
Harmony breathes the celestial air,
Peace clothed in kindness' rare,
Unfolds the umbrella of utopic care.

Of magical ideals, dreams spun high,
Beneath the rainbows of the boundless sky,
In the heartland where love does lie,
Unfolds the umbrella, wishes fly.

A sanctuary for souls that seek,
For the brave, for the meek,
In the land of the magical mystique,
Unfolding the umbrella, the utopia we seek.

Dialogues with the Dust

In the chambers of the past that rust,
Engage in dialogues with the dust,
In memories mired, truths robust,
Of forgotten tales and ancient trust.

Whispers echo across sands of time,
Each grain a story, each word a rhyme,
In the heart of solids, history's chime,
Speak the dialogues, silent, sublime.

In the folds of aged parchment and grime,
Lays wisdom's whisper, the chime,
In the dialogues echoing, souls enshrine,
Lost in the dust, the echoes divine.

So listen closely, let the dust speak,
Of yesteryears strong, of futures meek,
In forgotten tales, truth we seek,
Dialogues with the dust, wisdom's peak.

The Alabaster Archives

Within the hushed halls of marble bright,
Where secrets linger in the cool, crisp night,
Spectral echoes of the stories scribed,
In alabaster archives, secrets hide.

Whispers of the past tread softly there,
In spectral dance upon the cold stone stair,
Spun by hands of ghosts in gilded script,
In the alabaster archives, time is slipped.

Twisting tales of love, of joy, of dread,
Every chapter, every word, finely thread,
Now all stowed away in silence deep,
In alabaster archives, secrets, they keep.

Inscribed in lore, for seekers to unveil,
Through the dusty air, mystery sets sail,
Here in the heart of the hallowed heap,
In alabaster archives, stories sleep.

Bygone Blossoms and Bittersweet Bells

Bygone blossoms bloom beneath the boughs,
And bittersweet bells chime the hours now,
A melody that echoes in the dell,
Where we once loved and lost, and bid farewell.

Crimson petals scatter in the wind,
In every petal, a tale of lover's sin,
Our quiet whispers shrouded by the knell,
Of bygone blossoms, bittersweet bells.

The moonlight's dance upon their velvet hue,
A stark reminder of a love once true,
They're silent sentinels of stories to tell,
Of bygone blossoms, bittersweet bells.

As winter's touch lays still upon the land,
One heart longs for another's gentle hand,
And in the frosty dawn a soft sigh swells,
For bygone blossoms, bittersweet bells.

Life's Lavender Tides

Life's lavender tide gently laps the shore,
Bearing stories of ebbs, of rises, of yore,
And with each passing wave that swells and recedes,
We keep creating, losing and finding our deeds.

Cast adrift on a sea of hopes, dreams, and fears,
Guided by the whispers of vanishing years,
Through pain, through joy, through laughter and cries,
We sail along the stretch of life's lavender tides.

Each day bears a new tide, vivid or pale,
Changing with the wind, strong or frail,
In tempest or tranquillity, we hold our ride,
On the undulating waves of life's lavender tide.

With every crest, there's shadow, with depth there's light,
The balance ever-present, day succumbs to night,
On this lingering journey, whatever may be tied,
We're bound eternal by life's lavender tide.

Wreath of Wishes

A wreath of wishes woven with dreams,
Glowing threads of hope in golden gleams,
Bedecked with twinkling stars, deep and wide,
In each knot, a prayer carefully tied.

Motley blooms of courage, love, and grace,
Intertwined in memory's soft embrace,
The heart's deepest longing subtly implied,
In this crafted circle, a wreath of wishes tied.

Bathed in moonlight, under the night's watchful eyes,
The wreath resonates with silent sighs,
Each wish a beacon, our spirit's guide,
In the celestial wheel, the wreath of wishes, tied.

Every day dawns with possibilities anew,
Awakening our dreams, imbued with morning dew,
In life's grand tapestry, brilliantly dyed,
We find comfort in a wreath of wishes, tied.

Chants in Chiffon

Cloaked in soft folds of elegant grace,
A dance enacted in endless chase,
With chants whispered with delicate twine,
In a luxurious trance of chiffon refine.

Sung low in the whispers of the wind,
Ballads of love in their hearts pinned,
Encased within the silken wrap,
A symphony performed on nature's lap.

An echo of dreams spun beautifully wild,
Chants nurtured as a cherished child,
A story written in silken pleats,
Under the moon, where love often meets.

Ever-lasting, profound and clear,
The divine echo lingers near,
Enrobed in radiant twilight's glow,
These chants in chiffon, a graceful show.

Cascading Cosmos

In a limitless field of cosmic cascade,
Celestial notes of an interstellar serenade,
Chiseled by the artisan hands of time,
A canvas lit with stardust sublime.

Galaxies woven in an astral ballet,
Stars strumming chords of the milky way,
In the obsidian theatre of the endless night,
Cosmic secrets unfold in plain sight.

Radiant jewels in a velvet dome,
Guiding mariners who daringly roam,
Cosmos cascading like a silent hymn,
A harmonious design, far from whims.

Such beauty held in the vaults above,
An opus of the universe's love,
In the infinite rhythm of stars, we're immersed,
In the awe-inspiring tapestry of the cascading
universe.

Patterns of Poppies

On the green expanse, poppies make their stand,
Dancing wave-like across the gently rolling land,
A brilliant orchestra of crimson and gold,
Sketching patterns of stories yet untold.

Each petal, a verse in nature's song,
Where innate elegance and grace belong,
Unraveling their core in the morning sun,
Patterns of poppies, second to none.

Under the sapphire canvas of the dusky glow,
Amidst wild winds that whisper slow,
The poppies reverberate with the day's tune,
In the calm lullaby of the rising moon.

Painted in hues of the setting light,
Patterns that spark the poet's plight,
Poppies, in their transient bloom,
Craft intricate melodies that forever loom.

Shadows Shaped in Silver

A parade of shadows, shaped in silver,
On a moonlit dance, they whisper and quiver,
Moving in tandem with the ebbing night,
Underneath the starry blanket's ight.

Softly they stretch, gently they sway,
Carving mystical figures in their ghostly play,
Strung under the magic of Luna's trance,
In the tender darkness, they court and prance.

In the echo of the owl's serene hoot,
And the cricket's rhythm ringing astute,
With each progression of Luna's sphere,
In silver and shadows, stories appear.

As the dawn intrudes with its radiant sheen,
In the awakening morn, no shadow is seen,
The nocturnal ballet into memory fades,
In silver-etched shadows, where endless spectra
wades.

Forgiving the Fault Lines

Beneath the moon's quiet, quizzical glare,
Fissures of fear, forgotten, lay bare.
Hold not grudge, but in strength confide,
For even stars have scars they hide.

'Spite their faults, our hearts align,
To the rhythm of time, a tender sign.
Thorns of resentment, let us unwind,
In the calculated chaos, comfort find.

Gather your courage, embrace the cracks,
They're but life’s undeniable tracks.
Traced by history, inked in pain,
Forgiveness turns all loss to gain.

Do not dread the seismic shift,
Let love’s quake gently lift.
Through darkness, emerge the divine,
In forgiving, we breathe, we realign.

Savage Strength of Silk

Silk threads in moonlight softly weep,
Unseen strength in their whisper keep.
On a dance with the wind, unarmed, unbound,
The savage strength of silk is found.

Gossamer dreams spun into a prism,
In each strand breathe unspoken wisdom.
In delicate defiance against the storm,
The essence of endurance, in frailty, forms.

Doused in dawn or dusk, a labyrinth unfurls,
The language of life in a dance gently swirls.
Never mistake softness for weakness slight,
For even the softened silk outlives the night.

In the evening's velvet, secrets are spun,
The savage strength of silk, never undone.
In fragility finds fierceness, courage uncloaked,
For in the finest thread, robustness is evoked.

Honeyed Horizon of Hope

Shadows of yesterday creep and drape,
The morning sun, in mist's soft cape.
From dawning grey, a honeyed hue grows,
The horizon hints hope in poetic rows.

In each plaque of gold, a tale to weave,
Of quiet resilience, reason to believe.
The sky opens, an endless expanse,
Lit by hope's irrepressible dance.

Day after day, light on dark encloses,
Life's symphony in a cycle composes.
In the hush of dawn, dreams uncoil,
On the honeyed horizon, hope toils.

Let this be your sanctuary, your cosmic cope,
The relentless rise of a radiant hope.
In every sunrise, a sweet copyhold,
The honeyed horizon of hope, bold and gold.

Queen’s Quill

In the solace of silence, the Queen’s quill finds voice,
With every stroke, the pages rejoice.
Inking wisdom on parchment, lines pave,
Chronicles of courage, for the brave.

Her quill, the scepter, rules the white realm,
Pierces the silence, dons the helm.
Each word a jewel, tales untold,
The Queen's quill, in verse, warrior bold.

Laureate of longing, architect of dreams,
She tunes the sea to the moon's beams.
Queen of her castle, she pens her will,
Legends of love, by the Queen's quill.

Invisible ink of insight, decoded by few,
A labyrinth of language, verity's pure hue.
Scripting solace, a script untill,
Hear the whisper of the Queen’s quill.

Hidden Harmonies

In unseen corners of the world we dwell,
Soft whispers shrouding each clandestine spell,
A symphony hidden ‘neath midnight's veil,
Our secret songs on night's sweet zephyr sail.

Through silent echos, in shadows they bloom,
Harmonies born in secrecy's womb,
In heart's deep chambers, they’re softly unfurled,
Those hidden harmonies that shape our world.

Patterns of the Past

In the fabric of time, tales are woven,
Each thread a secret, silently spoken,
Through woven patterns of the yesteryears,
We glimpse joy, love, hope, sorrow, and fears.

Quiet stitches of events long past,
In memory’s tapestry held fast,
Our past is mapped in every suture,
We are who we are; by time's architecture.

Sapphire Sojourns

On a ship of dreams, we drift and glide,
Underneath the sapphire's velvet tide,
Across moon-kissed waves of tranquil bliss,
This voyage of dreams, in darkness, exists.

Sapphire sojourns on oceans serene,
In dreams are realities unseen,
Adrift on sleep’s star-speckled expanse,
In sapphire sojourns, our souls learn to dance.

Velvet Voices in the Void

In the void, velvet voices do dwell,
Their silent stories longing to tell,
Like echoless whispers in empty air,
Though unheard, they're always there.

In the nothingness, they weave their song,
Invisible threads, both short and long,
Velvet voices, in emptiness bide,
In the void, they speak; silence, their guide.

Rosy Reaches

Beyond the corner, where the roses bloom,
In the light of the silver moon,
Where dreams are woven on a loom,
And lives stitched by Fortuna's boon.

In these rosy reaches of mirth,
Where love is born and given birth,
Every man knows his own worth,
And happiness isn't confined to earth.

In petals of pink, secrets unfurls,
Like whispered words between boys and girls,
Casting delicate, crimson pearls,
Into the heart where desire twirls.

Sublime Shadows

In the folds of the evening, shadows fall,
Like quiet whispers, they softly call,
Carrying secrets, big and small,
In their cloak, they wrap us all.

They dance in corners, amidst the bleak,
To frightened hearts, they softly speak,
A solace for the strong, the meek,
The hidden language, the shadows squeak.

As night arrives with silent herald,
From day's disguise, truth is unraveled,
The shadows show a world dazzled,
In their silence, we are cradled.

Velvet Verses

Verses spun in velvet night,
Filled with stars, mystic and bright,
Speak of love, fear, joy, and fight,
The poet's soul in words alight.

Ruled by rhyme, meter and beat,
Each line a heart's soft, gentle bleat,
On life's wide stage, discrete yet replete,
In velvet verses, life and art meet.

A hymn, a dirge, a solace, a scream,
Every verse a waking dream,
In flowing words, emotions stream,
In velvet verses, we redeem.

Papillion Parables

Like the papillon spreads its wings,
To the tune that the morning sings,
Each flutter a story brings,
On the wind, it gently swings.

Born in husk, bound and confined,
To its fate, not resigned,
It transforms, leaves behind,
The old self, no longer enshrined.

In the dance of life's parable,
The butterfly's flight, so admirable,
A testament to change, durable,
The papillion parable, it's inscrutable.

Majestic Memoirs

Whispers of forgotten tales, beneath the brimstone sun,
Their glow of gallant glory, as stars that never run.

In the shadows, secrets sleep, tangled in time's tombs,
Awake by wisdom's whisper, they bloom in midnight's womb.

On parchment paths, in inked impressions lie,
A tapestry of time, painted in the sky.

Verses veiled in vanishing vapours, velvety and profound,
In the book of eternal echo, majestic memoirs are found.

A Handful of Honeysuckle

Under the honeysuckle moon, whispers weave a lulling tune,
In dreams, they dance, defying day, cradled in the crook of June.

Buds burst open, secrets shed, a tangle of honeyed hues,
Petal promises, soft-spoken, sewn in morning dew.

Fragrant kisses kindled, in tangled tendrils twine,
In woven whirls of wild, an intoxicating wine.

A stardrop's siren song, sewn into night's soft quilt,
Plucked from the heart of honeysuckle, woven into wilt.

Odes to Orchids

Dressed in veils of velvet whispers, orchids open in dawn's glow,
Bathing in the morning mist, weaving dreams from shadows.

Their petals paint promises, delicate and divine,
Each a whispered sonnet, scribed by the hands of time.

In the heart of the moonlight, they keep the night's refrain,
In folds of floral silk, secrets silently remain.

Brushed by the breath of twilight, in subtle light unfurled,
An ode to fragile orchids, the poetry of the world.

Drawing Dawn from Darkness

Undressed by the fingers of night, stars scatter into song,
Beneath the veil of velvet sky, whispers of twilight throng.

Candlelight weaves shadow lace, on the loom of the moon's embrace,
In silent silver sonnets, the night's enchantment trace.

From the inkwell of infinity, night sketches dreams unseen,
On the canvas of quietus, brushed in shades of serene.

Awakened by the aurora's touch, the night sheds its starlit shroud,
From the font of the darkness, emerges the dawn, bright and proud.

Through the Porcelain Dawn

Sunlight splinters on the dew kissed lawn,
Far from the maddening urban yawn,
Peeping through the porcelain dawn's crack,
In a world where magic's never lacked.

Whispers echo in the rustling leaves,
Chronicles of love, loss, and hearty heaves,
In the tapestry of dawn's whispering light,
A panoramic story takes its flight.

Dawn's sweet magic in every sunrise seen,
A testament to life, its joys, its routine,
Waves of warmth in times dark, forlorn,
Embracing tales of the porcelain dawn.

Portrait of an Ageless Maiden

Her eyes, windows to unending tales,
Her heart, an ocean where love prevails,
A timeless maiden, age defies,
In her gaze, a universe lies.

Threads of time weave her lyrical lore,
Etching shadows of yesteryears, adore,
A portrait painted in time's subtle sand,
Infinite tales traced by a tender hand.

Wisdom lines in the corners of her eyes,
Yet, her spirit, ever spry, never dies,
Wrapped in the shroud of time's golden hours,
Blooms the ageless maiden, like unfading flowers.

The Memoirs of Motherhood

In the silent sighs of a sleepless night,
In her lullaby's gentle, caring might,
Unravel the memoirs of motherhood,
Tales of courage, narrated, understood.

The first steps she guides, and tears she dries,
In silent sacrifices that never belie,
Her love, a harbor in the fiercest storm,
In her embrace, weary hearts find their form.

The bravest battles fought and won,
In the heart of a mother, for her son,
In her memoirs, etched in time's sweet hood,
Unfurls the story of undying motherhood.

Vanishing Veil of Vanity

Basking in the morning's fleeting plea,
Beyond the vanishing veil of vanity,
A truth emerges from the rising tide,
Where one's true self choose not to hide.

Clothed in colors of the primal dawn,
Vanity's costume, slowly unadorned,
Beneath the mirror's unflinching gaze,
Stands a soul, undaunted, ablaze.

Stripping off the layers of pretention's deceit,
Where truth and self in silence meet,
In unveiling of the vanity's veil,
In naked truth, we beautifully prevail.

Gentle Whispers of the Willow

Under the keep of the weeping willow’s arms,
Its gentle whispers birth midnight charms,
Murmuring stories of lost time and space,
Cloaked in emerald hues and dripping lace.

Reaching forth, an intricate ballet,
Their delicate dance at the break of day,
Tracing shadows on the silver stream,
In the shimmering light of a dreamy beam.

Resilient even when storms do roar,
Alluring beauty that one can't ignore.
The willow's whispers, a siren's song,
Echoing gently, all night long.

The Lilac Laced Letters

Fragrant lilacs scent the parchment pure,
Ink dipped in love, intentions sure.
Letters laced with lilac wishes,
Each word a soft, silk-spun kiss.

Black quill dancing on lilac-scented paper,
Delicate as the morning's first vapor.
In poetic prose and flowing script,
Every emotion subtly slipped.

These lilac-laced confessions of love,
Soar on the wings of a silver dove.
Words imbued with blossoming hues,
A story of love the heart peruses.

A Symphony in Sahara

Beneath the hearth of the blistering sun,
Where the gold of Sahara is spun,
Rhythm of sands in arid sea,
Compose a silent symphony.

Stars like notes flung across the sheet,
Where earth and sky in twilight meet.
Gentle winds strum an ancient tune,
Casting shadows under the moon.

The mirage weaves a hazy sonnet,
A tale sung by the dervish comet.
In Sahara's vast and aching expanse,
Life and music continue to dance.

Blossoms in the Blizzard

Blossoms bloom in the teeth of the blizzard,
Unwavering, the winter they've weathered.
In snow-kissed fields, under the iron-grey sky,
Courage and beauty in harmony lie.

Peeking through the snow, a burst of color,
Against the frost, they lean on each other.
Petals against the silhouettes of snow,
In the biting cold, a defiant glow.

Blossoms blooming under winter's might,
A testament to love's enduring light.
This evergreen tableau of blizzard and bloom,
A reminder that love always finds room.

Sprinkling Stardust

Under velvet covers of the endless night,
Each star a dream in celestial night,
I scatter the stardust, so bright, so light,
A cascade of wishes takes flight.

Can you see the cosmos' gleaming might?
In every fold of the nocturnal sight,
In every sprinkle of the cosmic light,
The stardust dances with titan's might.

In the silent whispers of the night,
In every dream that takes flight,
There lives a legend of stardust's might,
An endless tale under the enchanting night.

On Gingerbread Grounds

In the valley of sweetest delight,
On gingerbread grounds perfectly right,
Sugarcoated dreams take flight,
Beneath the moon's silvery spotlight.

Dreams of cinnamon, nutmeg in sight,
Crumbs of joy and laughter ignite,
Splendid towers of icing so white,
Bind the gingerbread grounds so tight.

From dawn till the star-pricked night,
Each bite unfolds a story so bright,
Of hope, of joy, of pure delight,
Roaring fires on gingerbread grounds in the night.

Paths Paved in Pearl

Beneath the moon’s gentle caress,
Lay paths paved in gleaming pearl's dress,
A path woven of moonbeams' finesse,
Where dreams are born and stories confess.

Under star-lit skies and the moon’s undress,
On paths of pearl, through night’s egress,
Roam tales of love, of sorrow, no less,
A symphony played at night's behest.

Through the paths, in dawn's gentle press,
Journey to dreams with no address,
Traversing paths paved in pearl, I express,
A painting of words, a moonlit finesse.

Stolen Sunshine

In the heart of the midsummer’s scene,
Lies stolen sunshine, golden and keen,
Hidden in meadows of emerald green,
Under the sky of cerulean sheen.

From every ray, stories unseen,
In each moment, in every serene,
The stolen sunshine, brightly preen,
Hidden stories in its warm gleen.

As sunsets infuse the sky with tangerine,
Stolen sunshine lingers in between,
The day and night, in twilight's glean,
A dance of shadows, painted in sunbeam's sheen.

Sunsets and Sapphire

When the sun kisses the sea, a tender adieu,
Sapphire shards shimmer there, reflecting the hue,
A spectacle of colors, of an evening's debut,
Crafting images, only a wizard can construe.

Each day ends, as though the sky weeps in rue,
Casting sapphire glimmers, on the night's dark blue,
Beloved stars emerge, in a twinkling crew,
As sunset's azure dim, to a silver new.

Sunsets and sapphire are but moments few,
Yet they paint our dreams, with a magical brew,
Every night they dissolve, in the dawn's fresh dew,
But their enchanting whisperings in our hearts accrue.

Lilith's Light

In the silence of the night, as shadows take flight,
Lilith's light burns radiant, relentless and bright,
Born of courage, wisdom, strength and might,
An epitome of resilience, defying the night.

Even when dangers assume, an alarming height,
Lilith's light perseveres, with resolute fight,
Through the tunnels of despair, it's the brilliant kite,
Chasing away the usurpers of inner light.

Lilith’s light, a celestial sight, the stars' delight,
It's the beacon guiding you, through a path so right,
Unyielding as stone, yet tender as twilight,
It's the dawn after the darkest and longest night.

Scarlet Silk Secrets

Concealed in the folds of the scarlet silk secrets,
Lie tales untold, in intricate packets.
Of battles fought, of love and regrets,
Of unwritten sagas and unpayable debts.

The fabric whispers, of passion and threats,
Embroidered with memories, that no one forgets,
Courage and shame, tied with ravenets,
Scarlet Silk Secrets, the heart never forgets.

Unfolding the layers, your skin it wets,
Chasing the shadows of ancient sonnets,
Secrets lie deeper, as the setting sun sets,
Beneath scarlet silk, truth and deception net.

Twilight Trinkets

When sun lowers her gaze at the end of the day,
From twilight trinkets, magic begins to play,
Silver whispers echo through the milky way,
Showering the world with a soft, moonlit gray.

Twilight trinkets, concealed as dull everyday,
Reveal their charm, as night carries the day away,
They glitter, they glisten, they dance, and they sway,
Enchanting the beholder, in an entrancing ballet.

As gloaming seeps, the world becomes their prey,
Hamilton's moons, and the galaxies' spray,
Through umbral charm, they keep darkness at bay,
Twilight trinkets, night's subtle, gentle display.

Obsidian Oceans

Beneath the star's refractory light,
Shimmering an ebony bright,
The obsidian ocean braves the night,
A world hidden from mortal sight.

The celestial gleam on the water's skin,
Mirrors the dreams that awaken within,
Casting shadows deep as sin,
In a battle that darkness cannot win.

Embracing waves beneath the midnight veil,
Upon the moon's soft-tinted trail,
Unseen mysteries do not pale,
In the obsidian ocean's tale.

The story told by the evening tide,
In a voice as deep as it is wide,
From which the ancient secrets hide,
In the obsidian ocean's stride.

Daisy's Dream Domain

In Daisy's realm of lullaby and lace,
Where dreams are spun with delicate embrace,
Where everything spins at its own pace,
Within this world, Daisy found her place.

In luscious green and petal white,
Under the moon's soft silver light,
The tranquil hours of the night,
Are Daisy's footsteps, feather-light.

She dances through the emerald dew,
To the rhythm that the night knew,
In a sky of the deepest hue,
Daisy's dreams are coming true.

A world pauses at twilight's seam,
Caught between wakefulness and dream,
Where all is not as it may seem,
In the tapestry of Daisy's dream.

Of Moonlight and Matriarchs

Upon the moon's motherly glow, they bask,
Unweaving tales from memory's cask,
In a light that removes every mask,
Offering solace from the day's task.

Through yesteryears, they weave a tale,
Across the silence, female echoes hail,
The matriarchs beneath the moonlight veil,
Guiding the ships with their ancient sail.

Their whispered wisdom kisses the breeze,
Passed down through time like an aged cheese,
The moonlight illuminates with ease,
Preserving memories like a freeze.

In the constellation of stories unfurled,
Under the covers of the world,
The moonlight shines and is twirled,
In the stories of matriarchs, tightly curled.

Waltzing through Waves

Beneath a sky, painted twilight's hue,
Where the ocean meets the sky's blue,
There dances a rhythm, pure and true,
The waltzing waves were only a few.

Their pirouette upon the sandy stage,
Is an entrancing, timeless age,
In the sea's frothy, salted page,
They waltz away their quiet rage.

With each gentle caress to the shore,
The ocean speaks its ancient lore,
The moonlit ballet, forevermore,
Is the waves' siren-song folklore.

So they dance, with tireless zest,
Beneath the sun's fiery crest,
The waves in frothy tulle dressed,
In their perennial, silent jest.

Time's Tightrope

Upon the narrow thread of time we tread,
With hesitations of tomorrow's dread.
Leaving behind moments of yesterday's sorrow,
On this journey, no second can we borrow.

Moments fickle, they tumble and fray,
Each footstep marking a different day.
We traverse slow under the stow of strife,
Balanced precariously between death and life.

Yet in this dance, a magic unrefined,
In bitterness, we sweetness find.
Castles crumble, yet heroes arise,
Change is the only constant, the wise surmise.

So walk the tightrope with courage bold,
Just like a phoenix, born from the old.
Time spins a tapestry, woven with hope,
Upon this precarious, thin tightrope.

Velvet Victories

Silent whispers in the shadow's smear,
Stealthy footsteps that only the brave hear.
Much like a lion, prowling in the night,
Victory is earned, not given as a right.

On the velvet mantle of the star-streaked sky,
The owl's hooting anthem echoes its battle cry.
Every dream deferred is a triumph in disguise,
Fanning the embers where resilience lies.

To win is not to vanquish, but stand tall against despair,
To invest in the impossible with an unabashed dare.
In the face of setbacks, we should not concoct stories,
For within each trial are hidden velvet victories.

So venture forth, bold and brave, amidst these silent victories,
And in life's grand tapestry, weave your own histories.

Rhapsodies of the Rose

Soft petals bloom in dawn's sweet light,
A rose whispers lullabies to the night.
The rhapsodies of its scent, quietly compose,
An ode to love, in the language of the rose.

It blossoms in silence, under the lover's gaze,
An icon of beauty, in the simplest of ways.
A testament of admiration and humble prose,
Such are the rhapsodies of the blooming rose.

The thorns, they prick, yet they shield and guard,
The fragility that love, often leaves scarred.
Its strength in vulnerability, the world shows,
The rose, with its thorns, love’s truth unclothes.

With every note, of its silent song,
It says, in all harshness, love can belong.

Thorns Bridled in Beauty

Thorns of the rose, sharp and stout,
A protective armor, keeping danger out.
Their purpose not malice, but to defend,
The vibrant beauty they dutifully tend.

Beneath the petals' silky feel,
Thorns bridle beauty, truth reveal.
Harsh they may seem, but they only protect,
The delicate bloom from reject and respect.

Thorns in the heart, too, bear a similar guise,
In the depth of sorrow, wisdom can arise.
For in our pain, a strength is found,
Thorns of life, in beauty are bound.

So fear not the thorns that prick and bleed,
For within our hurts, blossom seeds of great deeds.

Footprints on Frosted Flora

Upon the pristine sheet of white blankness,
A tale told in ethereal sternness,
Footprints weave through the frosted flora,
Like secrets inscribed in timeless Aurora.

In the woods where the ghostly shadows play,
Markings subtly reveal the way,
To where imagination and reality unite,
Underneath the fair moonlight.

The crunch of snow echoes in silent pleas,
A beautiful chorus orchestrated by the freezing breeze,
In the fold of winter's grandeur vast,
The poem of the snow is lovingly cast.

So remember each footprint becomes a part
Of the untamed wilderness' beating heart,
For in nature’s majesty, we’re but a trace,
Leaving footprints on flora's frost-laced face.

Midnight Magnolias

In gardens lush and moonlight glow,
Bloom the midnight Magnolias in a row.
With starlit petals kissed by night's embrace,
They whisper tales in their silent grace.

Fragrant mysteries beneath the moon's soft light,
They dance in dreams, an opulent sight.
Unfolding ballads in the hush of the dark,
Where even the stars leave their luminary mark.

In the still of the night, secrets they unfold,
Of love lost, and stories untold.
Their fragrance wafts in the tranquil air,
A symphony of sentiments for those who dare.

Thus, beneath the canvas of the star-sprent sky,
Bloom the magnolias, bidding heartache goodbye,
In the depth of midnight, finds one solace,
In the silent serenade of their midnight grace.

Sentiments in Stanzas

Word by word, line by line,
In subtle whispers, feelings entwine.
Each verse a mirror reflecting pure,
Thoughts that are harbored, words that endure.

Pain and pleasure, joy and sorrow,
Woven within the lines they borrow.
Accents light, impressions deep,
In these stanzas, sentiments seep.

Life's essence within each prose,
From each considered word, a feeling flows.
Verses echo, echoing this dance,
The rhythm of life set in lyrical stance.

Stanzas written in heart's own script,
On pages of time, gently flipped,
Echo emotions in resounding bell,
In the world of words, where sentiments dwell.

The Telling Tapestry

Threads of time on life's vast loom,
Weave together tales of doom and bloom.
Each color a story, each pattern a sight,
Within the telling tapestry of day and night.

In the warp and weft of existence's design,
Bound are tales of yours and mine.
Shimmering in silken threads of fate,
Are tales of love, and joy, and hate.

Threads entwine in intricate ballet,
Each thread a character in life's play.
The tapestry unfolds, patient and slow,
As destinies are woven, in life's ebb and flow.

Weave well, oh weaver of the cosmic loom,
Tales of sunshine, shadow, and gloom.
For in each stitch, each thread, each fold,
A telling tapestry of life is told.

The Dance of Duality

In chambers where light and darkness bloom,
Behind the masks, in the hidden room,
Good and evil in ceaseless gyratory,
Dance, oh, Dance of Duality.

In dreams where truth and deceit convene,
In dual realms, all that's seen and unseen,
Sorrow's ardor, joy's temporary,
Oh, enthralling Dance of Duality.

In truth's mask, lies often hide,
In love's grip, hatred's often tied,
Oh, paradox of humanity's library,
Such is the elusive Dance of Duality.

In heart's ballroom, where emotions sway,
Where virtues flourish, vices play,
To comprehend, oh the necessary,
Unfold, oh, Dance of Duality.

Whispers of Wildflowers

From verdant depths, where lilacs grow,
Come whispers soft, in dulcet glow,
Their petals paint stories in fuchsia and sapphire,
Oh, sweet are the whispers of wildflowers.

In dales deep, 'neath the pickleberry tree,
Where bluebells muse, a symphony we see,
In meadows where dawn and dusk conspire,
Breathe in the whispers of wildflowers.

Where poppies bloom, secrets unfold,
Marigold tales of summer days of old,
Immersed in nature's choral choir,
Echo the whispers of wildflowers.

From the heart where blossoms of love aspire,
To the soul where hopes set afire,
In gentle waves, in every hour,
Springs forth the whispers of wildflowers.

In dreams awake, in memories' power,
Where silence speaks, at twilight's hour,
Oh, feel the rhymes of the Earth's empire,
Reside within whispers of wildflowers.

Graves of Grace

Where marble angels stand in lace,
Repose the souls in graves of grace,
Beneath the sky's mourning embrace,
Quietly lie the graves of grace.

Spirits gone, in Earth's hold captive,
Kept in memory, poignant, active,
Beneath the yew's embracing space,
Rest those in the graves of grace.

Where daisies bloom, in soft elegy,
Rests grief's quiet anthology,
In ebon ground, stars find a trace,
Herein lie the graves of grace.

In silent hymn, we commemorate,
Those from us, the world did take,
In twilight's reflective fireplace,
Glow softly the graves of grace.

The Wind's Lullaby

The wind hums a lullaby, in whispered refrain,
Through the dance of the leaves, in sun or in rain,
In midnight's cover, under moon's bright eye,
Oh, sweet is the wind's lullaby.

Through the cradle of willows, it gently sighs,
As dawn's first rays, awaken the skies,
A melody soft, under the open sky,
The wind sings its soothing lullaby.

With the rustle of grass, it softly moans,
In the hush of the night, in echoed tones,
From the mountain’s peak, to the valley nearby,
Resounds the captivating wind's lullaby.

From the celestial vastness, to Earth's cradle lie,
The wind’s verses traverse, far and nigh,
In the quiet, with a soft goodbye,
Ends the enchanting wind's lullaby.

Tapestries of Time

The moon weaves tales, a shimmering silver silk,
A tapestry of time, wine aged in cask,
On nature's loom, where memories intertwine,
In whispered verses, in hushed bark and rusk.

Glorious, grand epochs drift in twilight gleam,
Ever unraveling their enduring hymn,
So, listen close, hear of the love and bravery,
Etched in the whispers of the ages whim.

Captured in woven threads, the cries and the calm,
The symphonies of history in motion,
Of painted shadows, cast under a starry palm,
A tapestry of time, life's wide ocean.

Cradle of Creation

In the cradle of creation, under twilight's design,
Where wonders gather, laying roots over the chasm's line,
Stars gather dust, weaving a tale of celestial rhyme,
Shining bright in the darkness, in the silent passage of time.

Watch as each galaxy, born of a darkness that swells,
Blossoms into being, as if under enchantress' spells,
Under the vast spectacle, where chance and fate dwells,
In the cradle of all creation, where endless life excels.

The cradle rocks gently in the arms of the nights,
Casting stardust, in the rivers of meteor lights,
The birthplace of stardust, where the universe alights,
In the cradle of creation, witness such resplendent sights.

Dusk in her Dreams

Under the veil of the night, her heart softly sings,
In her dreams, she sees a dusk, wrapped in violet wings,
It caresses her thoughts, with whispers of twilight things,
As moonlight weaves lullabies, and nocturnal springs.

In her dreams, wildfire galaxies swirl and untwine,
Through constellations of thought, dreams and reality align,
Her heart belongs to the night, under the opaline,
Where dreams and dusk dance together, in a timeless design.

Barefoot, she treads under the firmament's seams,
Embracing the quiet solace, that in her heart teems,
She finds her truest self under the stars' gleams,
While the dusk unfolds gently, in the haven of her dreams.

The Pages of Persistence

In the boundless chronicle of endeavor and strife,
Engraved in golden ink, are tales of life,
Chapters of resilience, written in hardship's knife,
In the pages of persistence, courage is rife.

In the maelstrom of existence, where challenges bloom,
The audacious heart stands, eclipsing gloom,
Pushing through the struggles, resilience does groom,
Through the unveiled chapters, where bravery looms.

Logos of resilience, imprinted, they shine,
Enduring every storm, accepting no resign,
Carrying the torch of hope, act as life's sign,
In the pages of persistence, victory is intertwine.

So, journey through these pages, these tales of existence,
May they leave an impression, an indomitable influence,
Of courage and fortitude, of resilience and resistance,
To writing your own story, in the book of persistence.

Passage through Plum Blossoms

In orchards of blooming artistry bright,
Where plum blossoms bloom with radiant light,
Pausing beneath the spring's tender bower,
As petals flutter in the waking hour.

Cloak'd in snow and embellished by the sun,
A silent tale of the seasons spun,
With every blooming bud, a story scribed,
Where beginnings end, and ends are ascribed.

In sudden gusts, the blossoms flurry fly,
Scribing stanzas in the spacious sky,
A poetic dance, in time and space,
Of fleeting beauty and gentle grace.

Amid the plum blossoms, I find my rhyme,
In the passage of petals, and the passage of time,
In the sweet, soft whisper of spring's warm air,
The echo of verses woven with care.

Beads of Brine

Beads of brine upon the cheeks,
Telling tales that no one speaks,
Salty streams from wells unseen,
Flowing from places 'twere we've been.

Crystal stories etch'd upon thy face,
Each teardrop, a memory encased;
In the echo of laughter, the shadow of strife,
Each droplet, a distillate of life.

Yet, in our sorrow, we find a light;
Stellar sparkles in the night,
The beads of brine, beneath the moon,
A celestial story yet to be strewn.

Far from the seas of yesteryear's lament,
A testament of time well spent;
For in every drop, each salty crease,
Lies a tale of resilience, a testament of peace.

Rhythm of the Rain

Can you hear the rhythm of the rain?
In the rustling leaves, its quiet refrain,
Where droplets dance in the soft midnight's hush,
Each melody etched with nature's brush.

Each splash, each trickle, a timbre spun,
In the silent symphony under the sun,
A serenade of whispers in the Mother's heart,
Of every ending and every start.

In the orchestra of rain, we find our verse,
In the patter on thatch, in the universe,
In the dance of droplets, on a silent sea,
The rhythm of the rain, the rhythm of 'we'.

So listen, hush, be still, and know,
The wisdom passed in ebbing flow,
In the rhythm of the rain, our stories unfurl,
Carved in currents of this grand, orchestra world.

Wildflower Whispers

Wildflowers whisper in colours bold,
Touch of velvet, heart of gold,
In the whispering meadows they bloom and sway,
An echo of nature's harmonious play.

In petal prose, they share their lore,
Sweet tales of sunsets, and times of yore,
Of tender dewdrops in the dawn's embrace,
The wildflower's whisper, a tender trace.

Between leaves of green and skies of blue,
A candid canvas of vibrant hue,
On the winds of change, their seeds are tossed,
In the wildflower's whisper, nothing's lost.

Listen closely and you'll perceive,
The wildflower's wisdom, the truths they weave,
In the silent song of the passing breeze,
The whispers of wildflowers, carried with ease.

Shaded Silhouettes and their Stories

In a realm where moonlight speaks, and shadows twirl,
Their tales steeped in the hue of midnights dark,
Eternal players in the universe's swirl,
A life wrote in the language of the lark.

Seen through the veil of the sleeping willow,
Where secrets are whispered to the unaware,
They dance with the gust, careen with the billow,
Their life encrypted in the cool night air.

Turn your gaze to the constellation in the night,
Every star shining is a story they trace,
In the realm beyond, your vision alights,
Find your silhouette, join the timeless space.

Their stories unfurl, like a moonlit path,
The essence of life, of love, of wrath.

The Loom of Femininity

In the heart of a diamond lies her soul,
Endlessly sparkling, multifaceted and bright,
Each aspect whispering a story untold,
And her power illuminating like soft sunlight.

She weaves delicacy within her might,
Lustrous as the weft and the warp entwine,
In her heart, courage takes flight,
A testament to a strength divine.

In the loom she threads the stars of the night,
Crafting a tapestry of dreams in the dusk,
Her wisdom imbued in each silken strand's plight,
Her mettle encased in a shell of dawn's husk.

She is the tempest and the serene twilight glow,
The paradox of a petal and the echo of a roar,
In her warmth, life begins to grow,
Femininity, a force, a whispering lore.

Diary Wrapped in Silk

In the heart of the paper, memories reside,
Whispers of yesterday, bound in a featherlight touch,
Each entry guarded by silken strands wide,
Preserving the secrets that meant so much.

Ink trails recounted tales of tender trysts,
Of heartache and triumph, dipped in twilight's hue,
Sealed within pages by a gentle wrist,
A diary cradling thoughts, dreams and views.

A testament to moments, hidden in plain sight,
Harboured in the bounds of gossamer fabric,
Each word a treasure, every line a flight,
All tethered to the heart, binding and magnetic.

Quietly whispers the tale to those who dare,
In the diary wrapped in silk, a life laid bare.

In Incense of Iris

Upon the hearth of dawn, a flower unfurls,
Iris blooms, a song in flora's verse,
Her petals embrace the day, as sunlight swirls,
A symphony of dawn, in nature's diverse.

In the tranquillity of the morning dew,
Iris dances in the whispers of the breeze,
Her tender perfume sighs, a secret clue,
To a story intertwined with the birds and bees.

At nightfall, she bows her head to sleep,
Sweet scent of iris still lingering in the dusk,
Her dreams flow like a river, broad and deep,
In the still night air, a floral musk.

In the tender echo of her last sigh,
The essence of iris ascends, to the vermillion sky.

Marigold Manuscripts

Beneath the marigold sun, writ in code,
Dreams of Prospero, tales by the boatload.
My fingertips dance on parchment so old,
In the theatre of mind, stories unfold.

The quill, like a phoenix, traces its flight,
Unfolding mysteries from day unto night.
Through words of aged ink and endless delight,
In marigold glow, the world sets right.

Countless narratives in my oasis,
Steeped in love and adorned with traces.
In marigold manuscripts, existing spaces,
The spirit of past, present, future embraces.

Oh, marigold manuscripts, my heart's domain,
Speak to me softly, ease my pain.
Whisper songs of joy, of love, of rain,
In you, I am whole, no link in my chain.

Subtext of Sorority

In the warmth of shared secrets, our bond interlace,
Smiles exchanged in moonlight, firm as a brace.
Together we bloom, as spring flowers with grace,
The subtext of sorority - life's heartfelt solace.

Whispered pledges, etched in time, as with quill,
Laughter echoing, the hollow silence to fill.
Shared dreams, tears, in unity, we instill,
The subtext of sorority, a vow to fulfill.

Friendship woven in magical light so pure,
In the halls of sorority, love secure.
Bound by shared dreams, hearts that endure,
The subtext of sorority, forever to assure.

Oh, sisterhood bound by shared memory,
Through shared paths and discovery.
The subtext of sorority, no mere reverie,
Forever entwined, in endless harmony.

Between the Rainbows

Where sunlight and raindrops dance in delight,
Nestles a realm, bathed in spectral light.
Frameless in time, flawless in sight,
There lies the land between the rainbows, bright.

Frolicking unicorns, dreams taking flight,
In the canvas of soul, painted in white.
Beneath the cosmic glow, hearts ignite,
In the space between the rainbows, ever tight.

Where hope and love eternally unite,
Echoes of laughter, banishing the night.
In tender moments, colours ignite,
Between the rainbows, a tale so slight.

In the blush of twilight, in the moon's limelight,
The secret held close, woven in white.
A secret garden, in words so light,
A tale woven 'tween the rainbows, the soul's delight.

Solitude in Silk

In the recess of mind, echoes speak,
My solitude etched in, not weak but meek.
Threads of solitude, in silk, they peek,
An opera of the soul, for the unique.

In a chamber of hush, let silence leak,
Words whispering secrets in tongues antique.
A harmony carved, a ballad peak,
Solitude in silk, a narrative to seek.

The quietude's lullaby for the meek,
In whispers of dusk, let my spirit leak.
Within the heart's silk folds, secrets speak,
Solitude wrapped in silk, fulfillment I seek.

The solitude in silk, so sleek,
Promises kept, the tongue does speak.
In quiet sanctity, all else is oblique,
My solitude, my strength, ever antique.

The Muse's Melodies

Creativity, like a risk, silently takes hold,
From the heart's cavern, emerge tales untold,
Her whisper sparks the pen, casting enchantments bold,
The muse, my ally, in words pure as gold.

In the still hours, she weaves her golden thread,
Of stories and characters, the world she has led,
Her song shimmers, like a knight's armored stead,
In the muse's melodies, all worries are shed.

In parchment of thought, she sketches dreams,
Under the silent moon's ethereal gleams,
Through her song flows life's unending streams,
The muse, my guide, past reality's seams.

With the muse's song, I am set free,
In the void's vastness, I dance with glee,
In her melodious enchantments, I forever wish to be,
The muse, my eternal symphony.

Pearls in the Pool

Upon the mirror's surface, they softly descend,
The sky's tears, their sorrows they lend,
In each droplet's prism, rainbows blend,
Messages from above, to mankind they send.

Embracing the pool, their journey's end,
Reflecting the sun, their luster they lend,
Upon life's canvas, their hues they intend,
As pearls in the pool, their beauty commend.

In ripples they dance, on the liquid glen,
A ballet of light, in nature's den,
A quiet whisper, 'neath the willow's wren,
In the pool's pearls, peace we ken.

Jewels of the day, their stories penned,
To the heart of the earth, their secrets they send,
Each pearl, a verse, the cosmos it'll mend,
In its depth, life's meaning, our soul's best friend.

Lilies of the Late Afternoon

Unfolding in the hour of the softening sun,
Lilies bloom, their story begun,
In the late afternoon's hush, their secrets spun,
Whispering tales of days delightfully done.

Ivory petals embrace the amber light,
Resilient, through the day's searing fight,
Adoring the sun's falling, the moon's silent flight,
Lilies of the afternoon, a tranquil sight.

Bathing in the glow, they sway and lull,
Their scent, the air graciously does pull,
A symphony in white, when the day is full,
Late afternoon's lilies, nature's beautiful jewel.

Cradled by dusk, under twilight's reign,
In the lilies' petals, dreams are lain,
The late afternoon's lilies, will rise again,
Under the morrow's sun, by the evening's fane.

Spring of Splendour

Awakens the earth, from winter's slumber,
Takes her first breath, quietly, without encumber,
Untangles the melody of the lark and the plover,
The spring of splendour, life's artful plumber.

In her radiance, the petals unfold,
Each bloom, a story yet to be told,
She paints the world in hues of gold,
The spring's splendour, courageous and bold.

She beckons life from the sleepy glade,
In her soft light, shadows fade,
In a symphony of colours, the world's remade,
Spring's splendour, in a verdant glade.

In her embrace, life hums anew,
Under starlit dawns, bathed in dew,
In every bloom, her promise rings true,
The spring of splendour, an eternal view.

Daughter’s Dawn

In the heart's silent chamber, secrets nestled deep,
A little light springs, quietly it does creep.
An incense of dreams, from life's sacred fawn,
Blooms in the aurora, of the daughter's dawn.

A moment stitched in time, with love's sincere thread,
Where innocence dances, and pure joy is spread.
In these magic hours, as night capers on,
Awakens the enchantress, in the daughter's dawn.

In the realm of wishes, she weaves her tale,
While pixie dust scatters, on the moonlight pale.
Into the panorama of yesterdays drawn,
Grows the vision splendid, of the daughter's dawn.

Borne upon the whisper, of a lullaby sung,
In the cradle of tomorrow, hopes are young.
A star is born, in the heavens it will fawn,
Gleaming gently, in the daughter's dawn.

From Eve to Eternity

Born from a whisper, nurtured by the stars,
Journeying through cosmos, from Venus to Mars.
From the eve of creation, till life's curtains are drawn,
Each soul embarks the odyssey, from eve to eternity.

In the heart's sacred chamber, memories slowly churn,
Fueling the lanterns, for the souls yet unturn.
From the cradle of cosmos to earth's verdant lawn,
The celestial artistry, from eve to eternity.

The ballet of seasons, the minuets of time,
Each penning a stanza, in the universe's rhyme.
Beneath the night's caped dance, till the morning's yawn,
Carries the enchanting song, from eve to eternity.

Each spirit pulses, in the vast cosmic sea,
Bound by the infinite, yet yearning to be free.
From the dusk of existence to dawn's jubilant spree,
Weaves the poetic saga, from eve to eternity.

The Song of the Silver-haired Siren

Beneath the moon's soft serenade, in the silent sea,
Resides the silver-haired siren, whispered in glee.
With voice that lulls the ocean, and stirs the sleeping dawn,
Sings the enchantress, her soulful, sacred song.

Her melodies spark starlight, weaving dreams in the deep,
In silvered shadows dancing, where sea nymphs sleep.
Binding night to day, dusk to the morning yawn,
Echoes the enchanting verse, of the silver-haired siren's song.

She draws the sun from slumber, and lulls the day to rest,
In her song of ages, the universe is blessed.
From the caverns of the tide, to the skies afar and yon,
Flows the haunting melody, of the silver-haired siren's song.

The secret of the sea, in her voice is twined,
A timeless serenade, to the waves and wind.
Til the final grain of time, from the hourglass is gone,
Will resound eternally, the silver-haired siren's song.

Empress Entwined

In the heart of the enchantress, where dreams and desires blend,
Rises the Empress entwined, at the universe's end.
With galaxies in her gaze, and stardust in her prawn,
Reigns splendidly, the Empress entwined, till eternity's dawn.

She binds with silken threads, the night to the day,
And draws the stars in constellations, in a celestial ballet.
In her dance twilight trickles, like a lover's long-drawn yawn,
Dwells the luminous enchantment, of the empress entwined.

From her throne she nurtures, the seeds of the universe,
With her wisdom as the sustenance, and love that she converses.
Across the cosmos and time, through millennia foregone,
Echoes the golden decree, from the Empress entwined.

In her heart is etched, every tale and tome,
The spirit of existence, in her celestial dome.
From the twilight's tender blush, to the moon's silver swan,
Boasts the allure and charm, of the Empress entwined.

Jewel-studded Journey

Upon path of stars, we tread alone,
Each step marked with dreams we've sewn.
In shadowed echoes, desires intone,
A jewel-studded course to the unknown.

In the parchment of night, our tales thread,
Carved by where the heart has led.
We traverse terrain both feared and fled,
On this journey, only by ourselves, we're sped.

Through twilight's lens, the world's endearment,
Each arcane corner holds engagement.
In the current of dreams, our hearts' arrangement,
The journey wears a jewel-studded ornament.

Where the cosmos casts its spell untamed,
Our journey, in celestial light, is framed.
In the jewel-studded journey, we became,
The master of the game, no soul to blame.

Letters to Luna

To Luna, my thoughts sail tonight,
In orbs of words, and crescents of light,
My silent whispers kiss the starry night,
In you, Luna, my dreams take flight.

In crumpled pages my feelings fold,
In ink, my unsaid stories boldly told,
I send my secrets to the moon bold,
In chilled silver, our tales unfold.

Luna, to you, my dreams I etch,
In parchment fair and moonbeam's sketch,
A silent watch, none can match,
Beyond the terrestrial catch.

To Luna, my confidant in the ether,
Keeper of secrets, wisdom's breather,
In our friendship, we are each other,
Endless letters, stories uncover.

The Decibel of a Daisy

A soft murmur in the heart of the garden,
The daisy hums its tale, unseen, unhardened,
In the meadow's choir, it's a quiet warden,
A melody ripe, in life's verdant burden.

In whispers, it teaches of sunlight's kiss,
The symphony of spring, life's gentle bliss,
In its soft decibel, an eternal promise,
Of life's sweet nectar, the world won't miss.

Its language folds in fringed bloom,
Amidst the verdant, its voice finds room,
Its decibel echoes in nature's loom,
The hymn of life, in a daisy's cocoon.

In its gentle tone, a lesson bestowed,
To sing the life's song in the mood awed,
The decibel of a daisy, humbly showed,
The silent wisdom, in life's broad road.

The Mother Line

In lines of strength across my palm,
The story of my mother does calm,
From her wisdom, a healing balm,
From generations past, a comforting psalm.

Her story births in the heart of mine,
In the quiet whispers of the mother line,
Bearing the fruit of the ancestral vine,
Her legacy, etched in my soul's fine design.

Through the labyrinth of time, a legacy spun,
A continuum of women, from mother to son,
The threads of life, irrevocably begun,
The mother line, unbroken, spun.

In every beat of my heart, her cadence rings,
The mother line, a timeless string,
To her wisdom, my soul clings,
The enduring song, that my lineage sings.

Mirrored Matriarchy

In chambers where wisdom gracefully tamed,
From cradle to grave, these matriarchs reigned.
Through love and loss their strength remained,
In their courage, their children were trained.

A matriarchy mirrored in sweet lore,
Their tales of strength, of love, and more.
In the glinting mirror, see the battles they bore,
Feel their heartbeat, silent, strong at the core.

Through every challenge they stood tall,
A clear reflection of love's call.
Their legacy, a protective shawl,
A mirrored matriarchy, standing firm through all.

Beneath ageless eyes and lips of truth,
Safe in their memories, lies our youth.
Their lessons shape us, in spirit and couth,
To the mirrored matriarchy, we raise our sooth.

Daisies in Desert

Scattered whispers, the daisies fraught,
In desert lands, with sunshine, are caught.
A spectacle of resilience, beautifully taught,
Bounty blooms where once we thought naught.

Amid the vastness, a mark of grace,
Daisies in desert, thriving in any place.
In the unforgiving barrenness, they embrace,
Life's toughest challenge, with elegance they face.

Silent defiance from petals of white,
A testament to life's relentless fight.
Against sand and storm, they shine bright,
In desert's heart, daisies ignite the night.

About survival, nature here sings,
And in quiet corners, life always clings.
Impervious to pain its barbs may bring,
The daisy rises, the desert's spring.

Lace, Love, Longing

Silhouetted in lace, traces of yore,
Fragile whispers of love in every pore.
Fabric finely spun, the heart's decor,
In every thread, longing dwells, no more.

Yet in lace, as in love, there's space,
A gentle interweaving, of time and space.
The soft thread of longing strengthens the case,
Heartstrings tangle gently, in this heavenly chase.

Through the fabric of life, we view the stars,
Weaving stories of love, healing unseen scars.
Bound by lace, love, longing, in memoirs,
Blooming essence of being, beyond earthly bars.

For in love, and longing, is a subtle trace,
Of vulnerability wrapped in elegant lace.
The tender setting of the human race,
In lace, love, longing, we find our place.

Silent Shadows in Scarlet

Silent shadows dressed in scarlet hue,
Under a moonless sky, they quietly pursue.
Their story immersed, in mystery and rue,
A spectral dance, beneath the clandestine blue.

Glimpses of whispers, secrets they hold,
In scarlet enchantment, tales unfold.
Under the shroud of silence, stories bold,
The realm of shadows, in twilight, they mold.

In the abyss, shadows settle and dart,
Rendering beauty to the silent night's art.
Their dance ageless as time's old cart,
A foretaste of darkness, in scarlet heart.

Yet these shadows in silence have spoken,
Of lives lived, of promises unbroken.
Silent shadows in scarlet, a token,
Of unspoken love, as night's only beacon.

Printed in the USA
CPSIA information can be obtained
at www.ICGtesting.com
LVHW022303150923
758321LV00005B/179

9 789916 392416